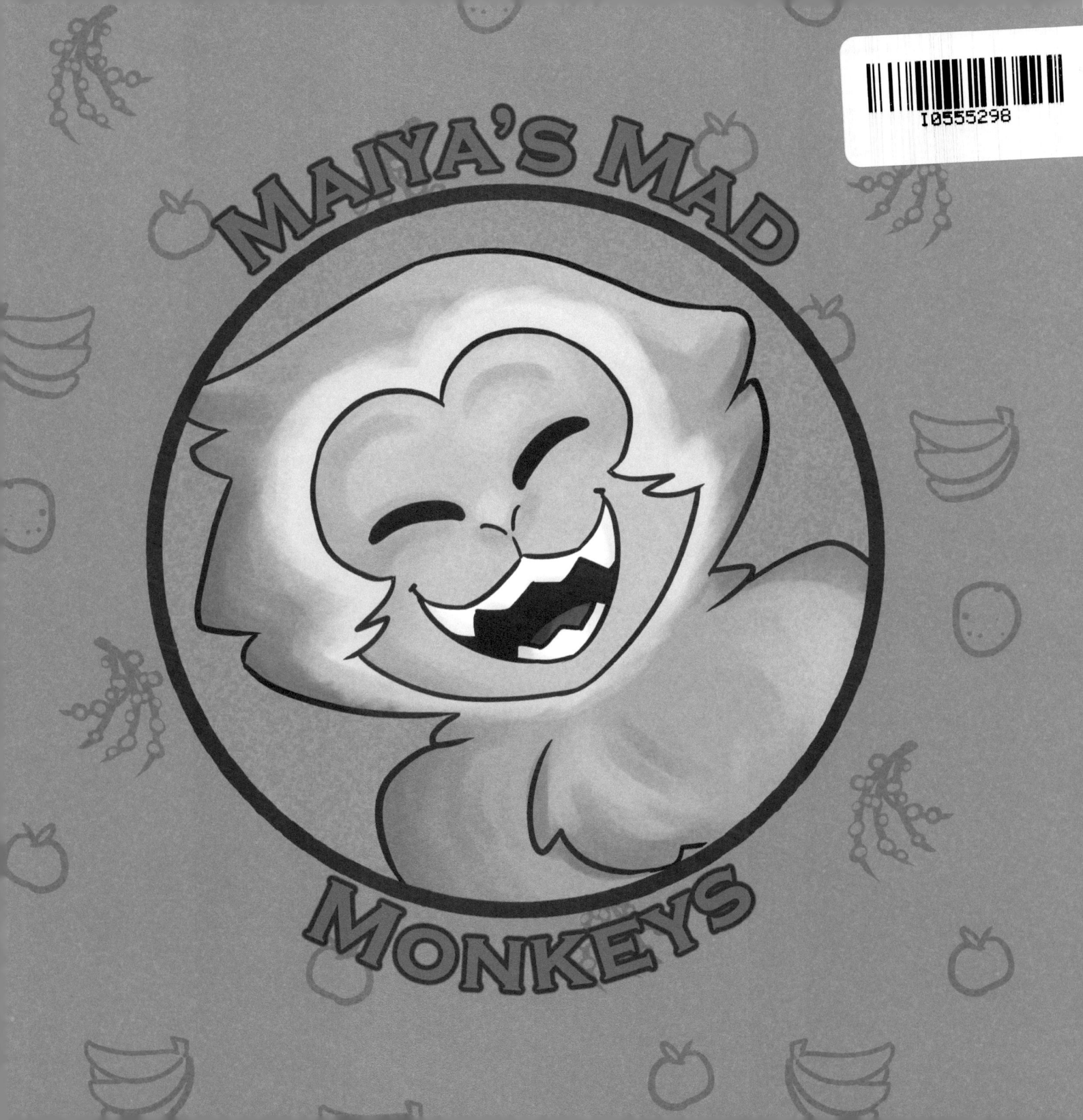

Dedication

This book is dedicated to our free spirited forever 10 year old Maiya Jean Marie Doherty whose lust for life and outdoor adventures never left her sitting still.
On occasion, when you would find her sitting down, she would always take the opportunity to cuddle up next to a loved one and read aloud one of her favourite books.
We hope you enjoy this book as much as Maiya enjoyed her favourite books and ask that you take this opportunity to cuddle up next to your loved one and enjoy this book together.

In memory of a mothers love for her daughter.
Harry Binnendyk

Maiya and her family had just moved into a village near the jungle forest. She was excited about the move to their new home.

As she explored the village the next morning, she noticed many of the neighbors frowning and complaining about the monkeys. The monkeys damaged their homes and trees while they stole food from their carts and orchards.

A few days later Maiya found one of the little monkeys with his hand stuck in a jar that was half buried in a mud patch.

Maiya then had an idea. A BIG idea. Maybe even a GREAT idea. What if she took care of the monkeys so they would not have to steal food from the neighbors anymore?

Maiya found an old pen with lots of room. She built a small fountain and added some pipes for the monkey to swing on. She placed apples and bananas inside the cage for food.
The monkey seemed happy in its new home.

The very next day, she found another monkey. It was trapped in a net and crying, too weak to escape. Maiya brought that monkey home also and added it to the cage.

Soon, the cage was full of monkeys, so Maiya built a larger pen. She built it around a large tree. Hung up a big tire and used the pipes to create a play area. She added a small pond and hung fruit up for the monkeys to eat.

The monkeys seemed happy. They chattered away and threw banana peels and apple cores at each other while laughing and playing.

As Maiya rescued more and more monkeys, the small pen had grown into a large enclosure. It was fenced around several trees, with ropes connecting trees and platforms together.

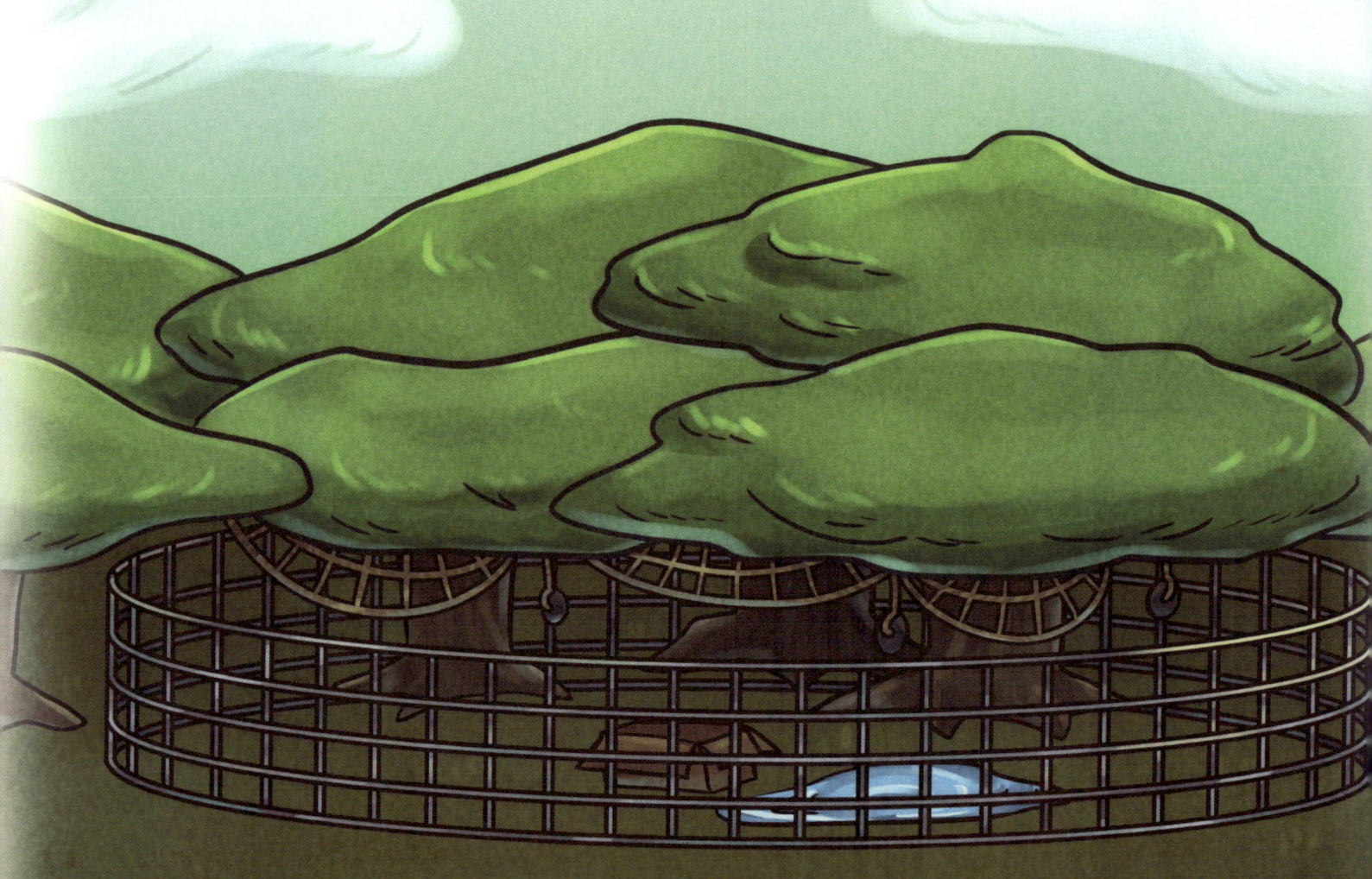

But caring for the monkeys became a lot of work. Every morning, Maiya had to buy large amounts of fruit from the local market. She used a big wheelbarrow to haul the fruit back to the pen, hanging it from the walls for the monkeys to eat.

However, some monkeys didn't like to wait. They would swoop in and snatch the fruit right off the wheelbarrow while Maiya tried to protect it.

Soon she didn't even have to look for monkeys to rescue. Each morning she found several of them already waiting by the door of the pen, chattering and demanding to be let in.

Later in the day, while shopping in the village market, she noticed that the people were smiling and waving at her.

"Thank you, thank you!" they shouted. "You've saved our farms and food. How can we thank you?"
"Um, you're welcome", a surprised Maiya replied.

But back home, things weren't as good. The monkeys had grown lazy. They would play and sleep in the big pen, content, because they did not need too look for food and drink anymore.

It became more and more difficult for Maiya. She had to get up earlier and earlier to haul multiple wagons full of fruits, nuts, and vegetables from the market to feed the ever-growing, ever-hungry troop.

Soon, it also became to expensive to feed the lazy, hungry monkeys. Maiya had run out of money to buy food for them from the villagers.

Then she remembered what the villagers had said. "I'll ask them to help feed the monkeys!" she thought. "They were so happy the monkeys were gone—they must want to help me feed them."

But each person she asked just laughed when she requested help from them to feed the lazy and demanding monkeys.
This made Maiya mad.

She returned home and threw open the doors to the monkey pen. "You can leave!" she shouted at the shocked monkeys. "I can't afford to feed you anymore! You need to go!"

But the confused monkeys just looked at each other and refused to leave the enclosed pen. They were used to having food and water brought to them.
Why would they want to leave?

But eventually, when the monkeys began to get hungry, one by one, they left the cage.

They returned to stealing food from the villagers' homes, and damaging the orchards, barns, and houses in the process.

The villagers would yell and swing brooms at the monkeys. But they just laughed from the trees and waited until dark to sneak in and take more of the tasty treats.

The next time Maiya visited the village, she was met with angry faces.

"Why did you let all the monkeys go?" they demanded. "Now they are ruining our lives again!"

NOW Maiya was angry too. "Then you should have helped me when I asked?" she snapped. "If you had, then the monkeys would still be happy in the pen!"

As she turned and walked away, one of the small monkeys was seen walking down the road toward her. It was chittering and holding out a rare piece of fruit to give to Maiya.
Somewhat surprised Maiya exclaimed "Well Thank you!" to the generous chimp.

Soon other monkeys began to bring fruit. In return, the villagers quickly learned to trade nuts and vegetables for the fruits. Some monkeys brought the wrong fruits, but they quickly learned what the villagers wanted.

Before long, the villagers no longer had to worry about the monkeys raiding their homes and farms. They had found a new way to work together.

Meanwhile, Maiya left the gate of the big pen open so the monkeys could come and go as they pleased. They swung on the ropes and swam in the pond. She often went out to the pen to chatter and play with them. Even children from the village came out to play games with the monkeys too.

Who knew that cooperation could be so fruitful?

Reviews

Maiya's Mad Monkeys takes real-world challenges and presents them in a way that's meaningful and accessible for young readers. My six-year-old was captivated by the playful monkeys and deeply connected with Maiya's efforts to help them. He felt frustrated when the villagers refused to support her, and genuinely moved when cooperation finally brought about change. It's a beautifully told reminder that true solutions often come when we work together.
Melody Sargent

Such a cute story, crafted in a way that makes it fun, not preachy. The pictures are amazing, ripe with beautiful colours that make turning each page a joy. I will totally buy this for the kids in my life.
Victoria Whitmell

Looking for more from the Author?
Steve's Stinky Socks
Frank's Frantic Festival
Hanks Horrible Hiccups
Gus Gets Gas
Bob's Best Bodyguard
Christmas Pants

They can be found on Amazon.

Want to keep up with other tales from the author?
Check out what's coming at
HarryTales.com

Need More? You can contact the author at: info@HarryTales.com

www.ingramcontent.com/pod-product-compliance
Lightning Source LLC
Chambersburg PA
CBHW041439120626
46547CB00002B/268

*9 7 8 1 9 9 8 2 9 6 0 9 5 *